Ripples

Poems

Dorothy Jardin

Artwork: Matthew Monahan, *Square Garden,* Koenig Books, London, 2014

Design: Brenda Juarez

Sage Leaf Press
P.O. Box 525
Los Olivos, California 93441
dgjardin532@gmail.com

Contents

Ripples

Bloodlines

Palm to palm, little hand in big crossing the street,
little hand on ropes big hands tied on a high branch
for a swing in his backyard.
Grandpa standing on his head, pockets emptying
change and peppermints little hands grabbed and kept.
Little hands at rest in her lap while big hand draws
a woman's profile and wavy hair, signs his bookkeeper's
fancy signature, *William Daniel Linnihan*, in linked letters
it will take years for a little hand to master;
so much easier to follow the melody of his song,
"If I had the wings of a blackbird,"
to follow his vision of balancing on a high wire
in a circus, big hands like feathers riding the air.
And skating, lines curving around obstacles
in the creek's ice, the same creek Grandpa
swam in summer, his body a reaching arrow
my eyes followed loving every inch of his precision,
not splashing or pretending to drown,
climbing out dripping and tipping one ear,
and then the other, kicking his leg to clear the water,
smiling and joining us on the picnic table,
water drops shining in his dark hair.

Sisters Of The Blood

Taught by nuns, Benedictines, Sisters of St. Joseph,
around eight or nine, I asked my mother to sew me a habit,
what their long clothes were called.

She whipped up a red skirt.
She knew better. She knew their habits were black.
"What kind of nun is that?"
"A Sister of the Blood," she said with a straight face,
knowing blood scared me, knowing I had not bled yet.

She had no desire for me to be a nun,
to not be a woman like her with a mink coat,
snakeskin high heels, in charge of her own house,
a beautiful woman with thick brown hair.
I didn't feel disappointed but amused and maybe grateful.
I could keep wearing good-looking clothes all my life
and be a dancer.

The red skirt could twirl though it was pretty straight
and tight enough around the waist that it wouldn't
fit me when I became a real sister of the blood like her,
like the nuns, who had to hide it, pray to Jesus
and the martyrs who bled all the way down to their feet,
rolled their eyes up and held their hands in prayer position,
which I imitated in the 4th grade and was corrected that
my palms weren't touching, that they slumped, rounded
like the praying hands of the school's statues
which were bleeding and ecstatic.

Much better to be a ballerina with a pink tutu,
satin slippers, a wide stage to spin on,
and a sleek male dancer to raise his arm
so I could dance circles around him
to a full orchestra, on television, and maybe in real life too.

Fur

(For B. J.)

Cold country girls—Pennsylvania and Minnesota
our mothers wore it.
We wrote Santa we wanted white rabbit muffs
for our little hands.
I was scared of the one I got for Christmas,
a wolf head in the center,
not what I longed for. The hard part of the package
could be the rotten potato my mother warned
my sister and me we could get if we were bad girls.

Late 40's my mom had a mink coat,
big shoulder pads, wide collar, way below her knees.
She remodeled it in the 50's, fingertip length,
slimmed sleeves and shoulders,
collar trimmed to stand up.

I have the coat now but don't wear it,
stroke it now and then remembering when my arms
weren't long enough to be straight down
on the back of the pew in front.
I cuddled next to Mom and petted
the fur through the long French sermons at St. Anne's,
and stared at the mink heads biting their tails,
hanging over the backs of the hatted ladies.
The black glass eyes worried me. I felt so sorry
for those little animals that could have been
chasing each other in the snow.

When it flooded one year in the Woods Addition
next to the Red Lake River in Crookston,
we had to hurry out of the house, get in a boat, and leave
before the water reached the kitchen.
My sister rushed out and knocked my waiting mother off
the front steps into the freezing muddy water,

3

her Persian Lamb coat and her whole self,
pathetic and furious.

Silent minutes in the rocking boat,
till we all laughed at once and the motor roared
and pulled us away to higher ground.

Thin skinned humans, we covet animal fur;
trapping, shooting, skinning, stitching;
parading wealth we had to kill to own,
while pampering our pets,
sliding into leather seats in our powerful cars,
fur lining our leather driving gloves.

Growing Up

I directed the show
the little show
on its little stage
        spotlight on my body
        where I imagined I lived
        dressed up perfectly
        ignoring the light designer
        curtain raiser
        stage sweeper.
I didn't question that I was supposed
to grow up to be somebody
let my light shine.
I didn't credit
the source.
I focused on people
their brightness   their shadows
ignoring my childhood love of trees
fur   the hollyhock's pink skirt   gold candle
the dancing webs rewoven daily
caught wings silent   translucent.

Deciding

Don't want to be an altar girl
or the priest
or the usher
        maybe the bell ringer
        but not everyday

maybe in the choir
        the bass but not the soprano
        not the organist but maybe the organ
        maybe the holy water fount
        or the Paschal candle

maybe the road or the horse on the hill
harnessed to the carriage with the fringe on top
        maybe the fringe
        maybe the ruffling breeze

the breeze
        definitely the breeze.

Reading Dr. Suess On His Birthday

Four hats on my head
  tall and wobbly
  pinned together
  so they don't tumble
onto Sophia, four years old, with cat ears
and a pink furry vest. She wants to know
where I live, and Frankie, 6, with missing front teeth
and white dots on her black coat, asks if I'm Dorothy
in *The Wizard of Oz* and I answer, "Sometimes,"
and tell them my girl name was Dottie
and my sister's real name is Sally,
like in *The Cat in the Hat*-- but first
raise your hand if you have read *Green Eggs and Ham*
and all the kids have so they can help me
and they do enthusiastically on "Not one little bit!"
and my hat hurts a bit
but holds on through *The Cat and the Hat* too,
which they know not quite as well but
one little guy gives away Thing One and Thing Two
in the orange box before I point out the loose hinge and let
them see the next wreckers on the long rainy day
when their mom is away.

After the mess disappears,
though we all did certainly see it and heard the goldfish
leap from its bowl crying, "No, I do not like it,
not one little bit!" just like the fussy guy
in *Green Eggs and Ham.*
I asked, "Would you tell your mom,
if it happened at your house?"
We all nodded, after barely thinking about it,
that yes, yes we would,
even this grandmother in a tall, stripped hat that wobbled
but didn't fall as she stretched out her arm to point at them
to finish the rhymes and say them as loud as they can,

"No, I don't like   , not a little bit   !"
but we do like   . We   . I do   !"

And Sophia hugged me and I hugged her back,
and Frankie thanked me and I thanked her back,
and that was that, so I took off my hat,
just a little bit sad,
but lots, lots more glad!!

Shopping With A Friend

Thrift store discount day
shifting through the racks
looking for a bargain
a possibility for your flamboyant friend,
her favorite color, her style, not yours.

But who bought, will buy
a white t-shirt with the word ORDINARY
over the heart?

You laugh and wonder who wants
to be declaring what is so
but shouldn't be. We are supposed
to be extraordinary.
That's what keeps us shopping to shine.
Racks and racks of struggling to be unique
and to belong to one group or another:
hippie, professional, preppie,
practical, athletic, arty.
Old identities overproduced, undersold,
never worn.

Too ruffled
missing an odd button
too short, dry clean only
closet full of plaid already
stripes in the wrong direction
too seductive
too dowdy.

A *maybe* held up.
        "What do you think?"
        "You, definitely, you!"
An embroidered pink silk kimono
roses and a tiger.

"Perfect, so perfect
for the true me!"

Why Did We Follow?

Why did we follow   the rock stars   the men?
Smart women   why did we paddle behind
in their stormy waters?
       The natural order? What we saw to do?

We were slow to know how
we could embrace the blue guitar
how our fingers could fan the strings
to back up our own voices
how our outfits could ignite an audience
our songs lead to greening
       not slamming down
       not endless trolling in overfished currents
       endless wars blowing up   poisoning   maiming.

Multiple stages now
women sparkling
opening their arms inviting the circle of voices
to harmonize   to call and respond
       nature's way being together taking turns
         shifting pitches and rhythms
         not losing each other in transitions.

How It Happens

A need   desire   mystery
starts a search   a gathering   figuring   trying
not knowing the time   the time it might take
to dine on the food grown in your garden
not knowing how many days before you can zip up
what you've cut out   stitched up
to read out loud what you've written
to positions your paintings
voice your proposal
shake hands on the sale
pass the legislation.

May be years dreaming   researching   revising
till a few people nod their heads   clap their hands
knowing how long a vision can take to spiral
its way to this moment.

The young watching
learning how to leap obstacles
welcome allies
to question: Should I?   Is it worth it?
Now what?

Lost in the dark
stopped at a crossroads
feet on seeded ground.
Which way is the light?
Eyes in all directions
listening inside and out.
Waiting for the wind
to whisper.

Path

End unknown
        imagined   surprising
maybe the only one to head out on
        to clear   stay on   abandon
others may have widened the path
        painted arrows   piled rocks
        branched off for an easier incline

the path may be lonely
        crowded with hurriers
            steep   slippery   narrow
            blocked with boulders
the path may be peaceful
        tree shaded along a stream
        flat through a wildflower meadow

desire   necessity   pull the steps   the deviations
fatigue remembers the twists   dead ends
the satisfaction
        aware
        here is where the path headed
            aiming for a high view
            a warming fire
            weather variations
            the welcome sound of the sea.

Confessing To The Mess

Confessing to the mess on our dressers
    only three of us around lunch
    but we bet millions throw down
    what they wore today and might tomorrow
        or wash mend giveaway

    tired quick to remove today before bed
    not folding but layering over days ago
        uprooting digging into in the morning
        hurrying up to begin again

    once in a while clearing the whole top
    so it's naked and admired
        but not for long
        until the company leaves in case
        they spy the mess: "Slopseedoe Junction"
        my mother would say

    our weekly allowance no longer withheld
        but a voice
        announces the name of the station

    a quick glance is enough to decide
        to retreat or attack.

Screen Doors

Some houses have sliding screen doors.
Some houses have none.
If your house has one you pause.
If your house doesn't a guest may be oblivious,
fall down: face, hand, wrist,
a loosened screen between whole body
and patio rocks.

And have to laugh or cry,
threaten to never return,
try to help clear the table,
trust a welcome.

After a while I will forget the fall,
being more in my house of winged visitations,
some biting, most caught in corners
by spider webs easily knocked down
by hand or broom, although they are helpful
house guards quietly capturing intruders.

But that screen humbled me.
What I do or don't expect can down me.
I have to slow my hurrying thoughts,
touch the skin of each threshold;
the thin protection problematic if ignored,
but impermanent like the plant's blossom
broken by my weight.

A Skin

Outside the back door a slender offering
a shedding only occasionally seen
saved and treasured

a young snake
thick circles where scaled eyes kept watch

long upper skin translucent ovals
the under skin jointed, wide rectangles
for coiling, for quick escape.

       When is the time the body urges release?
       Does it require
       rubbing against something rough?

       These tense days of rightful protests,
       what are we shedding while masked?

       Our skin sweats
       itches before words
       justify feelings

       before life pulses faster
       pushes loose the constraint
       of a past protection.

Do I Have To

Do I have to write another possible poem,
to search for a stone shaped to save,
rust rising to meet what broke off a white rock
an old river left
for my hand to find and study?

Do I have to tell anybody or myself
what I half understand,
to listen hard for a phrase in the pines,
an old memory of standing on the end of a dock
embracing a lake, round and shining
in its ring of swaying green?

Do I have to write to remember ripples coming toward me,
the sun above branches, of belonging
where I have never been?

Inky Hands

Tough to re-ink my black Parker pen, but I am insistent.
Its refill plunger sticks, hurts to push, chips fingernails,
but grudgingly nudges when forced by its own cap
to suck up more black so I can push its point,
hoping it will write.
           What is it I hope for?
           Sense? Surprise? Ordinary truth?

Sounds ooze into the crossed t's, looped o's,
scoot together to be words I have written before and
words sighing in the shadows.

Ballpoints, felt tips, pencils perfectly satisfactory;
for some, straight into electronic keys,
but I am old and fell in love with
fountain pens early on; the nuns' beautiful signatures
on report cards, my mother and father's matching
black and gold striped Schaeffer's.

So I have inky hands on a regular basis,
and a writer's bump on my second finger
and rows of black writing books
with a few dog-eared corners marking possible poems
to type up and revise.

In a little while I will slide into my walking shoes,
do laps up the road. Once muscles are trained
they repeat their action. So talking to paper with ink,
a habit rechosen, rechosen; a vocation I've answered,
loving the call, accepting reams of futile scratchings,
stained index fingers, smudged desk edges and

A few transformations
liquefied into language listening to its
rustling branches toss leaves into open air,

marking the ground with their heart shapes, arrows,
their articulate green fingers.

In The Middle Of It All

Tadpoles in the fountain
new pussy willows in vases
a migration of moths
another new leaf on the pear tree
the tall grass mowed in circles
to walk into   to return
peace in the middle

Despair a shadow
uncertainty a widening of eyes
Now what?   Answered by an empty road
the dinner dishes stacked in the sink

Hands in hot soapy water
scrubbing the roasting pan
hands wiping the sticky counter

Peace in the familiar
in the middle of it all.

Ocher Leaves

Ocher leaves litter the terrace
drift   scratch out their wills and testaments

not their last   their final   final
though shriveled   shadowed
accompanied by twisted wisteria seed pods
and their thin curved stems

their once green leaves   twelve
side by side   one on the tip
held on for months

not all falling at once
but when   nothing connects anymore

like clear intentions to let go
of youthful ignorance   adolescent anxiety
mature certainties

which seemed to be   how it is
until it isn't.

Raisins

Common as crackers,
little red boxes in school lunches,
smiling maiden with a basket,
which I am now,
so I have a jar in the fridge from the prolific
Thompson's Seedless by the front door.

I know the grapes are ripe when the stems dry,
the birds scurry away when we come and go,
and the clusters lose their lush tips and turn rusty.

I pick more than we can eat,
gift my acupuncturist and chiropractor
and friends who come to dinner,
and then I pick what's left and lay them
in a cotton woven bag on the outside sunny table,
turning them till they are universally wrinkled.

And then the tedious picking off of thin stems
while waiting for the rice to boil,
the fish to soften,
the tea to steep.

I cook a few with kale,
a few with almonds in ghee, turmeric,
rosemary and fennel.
They are barely tasted--concentrated sugar
in tough skin you have to chew with front teeth--
tiny, everyday generosity to slow down to savor.

Last Year Of Seventh Decade

Sunrises and sunsets, fog, afternoons of heat waves,
wind, and temperate weather inside my aging
joints and ego.
Outside and inside an ageless spirit.

Illusions fading. What forms and unforms
informs momentarily beyond the books
leaning on my shelves; the ones returned
to libraries, the ones not yet written.

My life seems to be attraction,
a need to play, be curious, perplexed,
grateful to be living on the edge of a sea
and in a valley of rounded hills and vineyards
in the company of love in a world of complexity,
terror, invention, awe, grace, opportunity, mystery.

I am a small part waving and watching,
my body knowing how to dance in shifting rhythms,
my mind narrating and planning, questioning
and calming itself.

Decisions

One of today's
    where to circle the outside chairs
        in the sun
        away from the recent gopher upheavals
        near the house not too close to road noise
        with some access to shade.

The legs of the chairs will sink unevenly
old gopher activity bumping the ground
        and how many chairs
        not all invited confirmed
empty chairs will represent the missing.

It will be the Solstice during the day
our Women's Group reflects on this year
what to leave   what to invite
and our seventies
        just starting
        or advancing into the next decade.

What matters is being able to move
to be able to lower ourselves and rise
        helping each other as needed
        clarifying what means the most
        the direction to keep heading
        changing when a different path
        requires adjusting to the uneven ground.

        That's what we have been doing for decades
        entering and exiting one circle after another
        singing a seasonal song and an old favorite
            "Tis a gift to be simple
            in the valley of love and delight."

A gift to be together all these years

trying to be our aspirations
listening to ourselves and each other
mirroring our graceful spirits
and our jagged struggles
  accepting what is so
  not all alone with sorrow or joy
  being loved
  supported
  seen heard
  held.

Fussing And Fuming

Having a fit
falling in
legs kicking the air
head in tar
fire stoked by talking itself into a frenzy
smoke whirling
choking itself.

Now what?

Splayed in ashes
a sacrifice to
which voice
preaching
demanding?

Which old scar torn open?
Which throne wobbled by which worry?
Which sympathizers armed and ready for retaliation?
Which subjects huddling elsewhere plotting?

Yes Means Yes

(Lara Schnitger, Suffragettes' City, Hammer Museum,
November 12, 2016 after the election)

Yes brave yes scared timid wild weak persistent
Yes child woman man elder
Yes wanting yes not wanting
Yes mixed separate not alone
Yes negative positive confused willing unwilling
Yes wanting to look good not look good
Yes to see be seen ugly beautiful
Yes don't want to reject and do yes to reject
Yes a mess not stopping not stopped
Yes ignorant wise indifferent passionate
Yes not finished yes chaos yes deciding

Yeses deciding
Yeses colliding not in the same state
Yeses in the same state

Yes to facing opening closing
Yes to yelling whispering silent
Yes to feeling solid not solid
Yes to trying to hold on
Yes to not trying to hold on
Yes to watching listening uncertainty
Yes to crossroads
Yes to wanting to run away
Yes to wanting to stand still
Yes to what is coming what is going away
Yes to knowing
Yes to steady to peaceful even though
Yes to
Even though.

Bird Brained

Not all birds bang into glass reflections
defending their territory.

The Spotted Towhee attacks windows
north and south, French doors,
car mirrors.

Must have a harder beak than other birds
who perch and dive but don't
repeat their futile strikes
to defeat themselves.

The lizards scoot into shadows,
though they are not seen in the bird's focus.

The Towhee flees when I shout
and wave like a maniac
but he returns, returns, returns,
a dictator
not knowing the unknown attacker
is himself, himself, himself.

Uninvited Dinner Guest

An uninvited dinner guest each of us brought
disrupts our tasting the fennel, capers, chilled wine;
our elbows up to push away his aggression, ignorance,
racism, corruption, arrogance.

We shout, shake our heads, so disgusted.
Our host sweeps her arms over the table
removing cluttered plates and him.
Enough of his usurpation of our peace.

"Who wants apple pie and ice cream now?
We sigh needing sweetness to coat our angry throats.

Dusk is purpling the sky.
Venus accompanies the half-moon
above the silent mountains.
The coyote waits to cross the field.
The owl cries her presence.

"Who wants a big piece? Two scoops? A little brandy?"
We sigh, rest our forks in the cream and crumbs,
sum up how we feel.

I'm resigned.
I'm scared.
I'm moving to the Bahamas or Japan.
I'm so damn mad.
I'm hoping we'll wake up. Wake up now!

We hold each other's voices, each other's faces,
in the darkening light.
Time for candles. Warmer layers. Going home.

Lizards rattle the fallen wisteria leaves
pushing up, pushing up, feeling the ground

safe enough, safe enough for now.

What's left of the uninvited
shifts in the fall winds, drifts on the uneven ground,
dreams he is the top of a pepper tree on fire.

'No More Chit Chat'

Too hard on
        steep ascent

pounding heart
loud breaths

someone ahead calling
        "Not far"

doubting it
        sorry stupidly agreed

legs cramping
        knee protesting
                swearing
                stuck in throat

whole body   old   old
        shouting "Quit! Quit!"

mad mind
        blaming rocks
        sun
        leader
        endless path

"Better be damned good
        at the end!

"Better be
        better than good!"

Maybe Hopeful

Possibly
      arriving from an unknown direction
       time location

Possibly
      a vision sailing like a penny
      tossed into a deep fountain
           water circling circling
           watchers reaching into their pockets
           for copper for silver change

      more and more shining circles
      below the surface
      nudging each other
      cross rippling.

Studying Zen

My Japanese pen at first did fill.
Its plastic ink cartridge when empty
could be pumped full again by dipping the nib
into the ink bottle and twisting the end down and back
maybe two or three times

and then it didn't fill
mostly air bubbles and a thin web of ink

so I brought the pen back to the bookstore
in Little Tokyo in Los Angeles where I had bought it.

A young man and a young woman immediately
stopped their conversation behind the pen counter
to listen to my problem.
We lowered our three heads over the failure
tried a new cartridge
the young man asking, "May I?"
the young woman offering a different pen
with the old cartridge which still didn't fill
so we tried a new cartridge
tried slanting
tried turning slowly twisting while slanting
tried a pre-filled cartridge which worked
so it wasn't the pen
tried the pump again
tried washing the pen
called the supervisor for another suggestion
tried a full bottle of ink with the new pump
and that was the solution.

No air can enter the nib's circle
the ink must be deep
the twist must be slow
attentive

polite
calm
curious
cooperative
grateful.

Spy School For Private Investigators

You can buy a fedora and a trench coat, or not,
but you'll need some memory pockets, no matter what,
and one of those eyeball-enlarging spy glasses
could be helpful when doubting vision
though invisible magnification is most useful,
an amplifier for shadowy opinions.

Prior experience is optional but
patience is definitely required and daily practice,
sitting still doing nothing but private investigation,
eyes open or shut, not judging if possible,
forgiving your habitual preferences and die-hard beliefs.

Slow walking is recommended, noting wobbly balance
maneuvers and leaning left or right, forward lurching
or holding back in the head and the hips,
heals hitting first, or after the toes fan out
to kiss the ground.

It's important to listen to birds, lawnmowers, tires, cries,
chuckles, running water, coughs, air conditioners, flutes,
the wind, what you say to yourself and to others,
and what you don't.

This school requires language study, some Japanese,
Chinese, Tibetan, and Sanskrit;
plus your own native vocabulary,
including foreign phrases learned in travel and high school:
Mon Dieu, Donde esta´, Bellisima
and languages without words:
body talk, music's variations,
visual composition, dance moves,
the internet's algorithms; cookies, twits, chats, blogs--
easy to be lost and confused—caught in a glitch.

But you've got to stay unperturbed, be kind while trying to
suffer less than usual and not blame, stab, trick, hate, quit.
No out in this school.
Everything is connected to everything else
even though some creatures seem completely oblivious
while others are teachers,
and they trade off so you
never know for sure what to ignore.

Pretty soon you don't know who you are,
think you were—or care.
The lizard's your sister, the mountain your mother,
the sky your mind.

You still have to eat, do the dishes,
make your bed if you have one,
chase your own tail and follow your nose
in order to graduate into
a less crowded space where it's easier to see and hear,
letting the clues come and go,
one case closing, another soon to open, so no hurry,
many tests, but no grades, no diploma.

Allow

Allow the apple to anchor in your palm
the arrow to narrow to air

allow open to answer
allow agitation
allow darkness to sing
to rearrange dust

allow dead leaves to whisper
drop shift rattle

allow the star in the apple
to be seeds in your garden
to be teachers

allow mysteries to twirl
beyond translation

allow not knowing how
allow how
knowing knows.

Everything Dances

Everything dances:
trees, humans, wind, dust, water, conversations;
always a dance, slow swaying, ecstatic arms in the air,
leaps, shuffles.

Trees usually stay in the same place on the dance floor,
shifting and balancing while rooted.
Do they prefer waltzes and tangoes to hip hop?
It's easy to imagine trees as humans like us
with arms and aspirations.
Do we feel as stuck in the ground,
free only on our edges, crowded or solitary,
bothered by squawking perchers,
burrowing parasites?
Do we prefer silent partners,
a chanting steady rain, slow love swooning?

Do we welcome a stormy symphony,
crescendos testing our resilience,
a knocking loose of old twisted weight,
too many repeats of the same prevailing winds?

What Is This?

Keep asking without answering
        comparing   explaining   liking or not.

Korean koan of presence:
        What is this?

How do I keep my hand from not raising to answer?
        To study silently what barely flickers?

To be in empty space without building
        a jeweled edifice?

If I name this escaping sigh a question
        and not chase it

Where am I? What is this patient
        curious place?

Stop

Stop stopping   trying to stop
what knocks   comes in snoops around.

Don't attack   push pick up   run away.
Be curious   hospitable.

Notice belly grip   jaw lock
the height of your fire   the arc of sparks
the sure voices   familiar plots
the snarling nightmare snouts.

Blow a temperate breeze out of a blue sea.
Invite the sun to melt your helmet
shield   your long sword.
Let them become a slow gold river
shaded by green
where birds perch long enough to be named
for their songs to be heard
to be answered.

Not Sure

Not sure "without hearing a voice intonate."
Not sure how to be sure where "Sure" stands.
      Half out the door?
      Arms crossed hard over heart?
      Head nodding yes, shining eyes eagerly agreeing?

Is the request, the question thrown, doubting assent?
Is it wanting an honest answer
      not a racket smacking back without a pause
      scoring a goal in an unscheduled game
      or a soon forgotten impulse?

A flat "Sure" sent on a screen
a small rectangle for response
      a cryptic emoji
      three dots
not sure if
hands in prayer or
cartwheel.

Some Days

Some days clouds touch the ground
for hours of loving,
catching up with family news,
welcome or not,
conversations continual,
sometimes heated sometimes sparse.

Laozi, the ancient Taoist, recommends *Wu wei,*
not expecting or rejecting what is other than it is:
rainy, hot, fogged in, windy.
Mud will be sticky, ditches wet, full of thistles
and milkweed, which butterflies need,
though we might prefer water lilies.

Clouds can be welcome without lamentation.
Clouds can thin and disappear without despair.

So many small frogs now announcing their presence,
so many mosquitoes growing their wings,
and the grass waving its green and stretching.

And I am questioning,
and accepting I am questioning.
　　　　Am I a greening field
　　　　bowing in the wind?

What's The Rush?

Running over the slow down sign,
        smashing it beyond unbending.

What's the rush?
Hair takes its time to grow long enough
        to braid, cut off, donate
        to Loving Locks in the name of
        a young one who ended his life,
             a rush to stop thinking about death.

        He's missing a romance, a reunion,
        a rest on a bench with a warm breeze
            lifting and lowering
            the fringe of hair on his forehead,

        his mind free of having to do something,
        to not think about
            hurrying up,

        a moment to watch a woman try to
            straighten out what's been run over
            too many times to fix,

        a moment to watch and understand
            wanting to fix
            and not jumping up to fix,
               to stop,
            back supported
            feet on the ground
            able to get up and go
               when the rush
               is over,
                   the way is clear.

Quiet

Inside a sweater drawer

a shadow under the patio chair

      a tarantula crossing a country road

minnows under a dock

      a closed book

      an empty white cup

a line of pelicans low over the sea

the slight curve of the horizon line

quiet not preferring what is coming   going

staying awhile.

A Well-Knit Life

Attention entering each space
care looping yarn between needles
slipping off completely
stitch after stitch
stitch after stitch
tension not too tight
too loose

even so
caught on unseen edge
pulled askew
unraveled

even though well-knit
opened in darkness
toothless hatched eggs sawing through the grid
voiceless jaws savoring a sticky spot
the hole ignored or rewoven with thread
closest to the lightest hue

a well-knit life can still sag around the neck
thin in the elbows
ball up from arms rubbing against ribs
can still be smoothed
its familiar scent treasured.

Why Do The Doves Sound Mournful?

This new mantra, "clear   peaceful"
hasn't changed their minor key.

Who's pitched them to lament
while being symbols of peace
and the Holy Spirit?

Hope is for the future.
After centuries of warring stupidity,
we hope, but not with exaltation.

From the doves' high perches
they must see how we could settle down,
know we are one another,
despite our coloration,
our red convertible,
our high-wheeled pick-up.

And who is still tossing beer cans
out their windows,
muscling a crunch
which bends the blue label
but does not make it disappear?

And who is that woman
picking up feathers and abandoned cans?
She talks to the doves
as though they are her relatives,
translates their warnings and calm statements:
"Hurry up   hurry up."
"Loved   loved   loved."
"Wake up   wake up   wake up."

Continuing Conversation

Though the earth
fell away from the sun
and the moon
dislodged from the earth,
their continuing conversation
raises and lowers the seas.

Winds conspire over tidal currents.
Waves rise and rush to slam shores,
indifferent to scurrying creatures.

Cliffs thought safe loosen their boulders.
Rocks flatten in the pull and push of the surf,
become sand and pebbles.

What was frozen thaws.
Where fish flourished, nets are empty.

How old is this unrest,
this heated discussion?

Long before humans settled
with their preferences,
dramatic fluctuations buried our histories,
so so so slowly
so suddenly.

The islands now losing their edges
were mountains of fire.

      How do we join this cosmic conversation?
      Pointing our fingers in blame?
      Hollering ourselves hoarse?
      We are guests in this wild household,
      needing to clean up after ourselves,

have our suitcases ready, our eyes and ears open,
our creativity in gear.
Our conversations must be deep and wide,
our translators able to speak algae, oak, owl,
salmon, pelican, bee, river, coral, dove, child.

Wisteria Seed Pods

September they twist   pop
        throw their flat seeds into the air
            the lavender   euphorbia   aloe

Big as dimes   dark as chocolate
        most land on the patio's cement
            shrivel in the sun   not becoming
                new flowering vines

Winter is short in California
        nature a year-round-curriculum requiring
            observations   tests

If you don't pick up the pods
        you step on them   either
            bend   bend or sweep   sweep

I collect and treasure them awhile
        pet the sage suede   fit my fingers into
            the ivory indentations   float them in the
fountain   hand them to admirers.

Art is everywhere
        it's our nature to be magnificent

            like the full blooming wisteria attracting
            bees to continue being what it is
            like us flourishing
            flinging husks along with our seeds
            being mulch in our own shade.

Pearly Everlasting

Pearly everlasting browns the vase's water
      while opening their yellow centers
      their white fringe petals.

The pearls point until they fully press
      into the white tips and spring back
to become a balm a butterfly has blessed.

Herbalists know the right proportion
      of alcohol, darkness, and time
      to brew a tincture
      to ease a cough, tame a sneeze.

What else do I live near that can ease
      what ails me?

I know their beauty calms me
      and their woody scent
      stalwart height
      abundant branching pearls.

Drinking flowers is appealing.
      Maybe my wings will sprout.

Maybe human wings are ideas
      the heart advises hands to gather
      from ground kept sacred.

Solstice Morning

(For Cynthia)

Not the darkest day yet
sun through the prism   blue yellow red
on the wisteria shadowed wall.

"Wonders abound" my friend wrote
on a Christmas postcard of a seashell
no exclamation mark.

The shell has another shell stuck in it
and now spirals in an Oxford Museum.

Someone found it and saved it.
It kept showing up, some tide pushing it
into wondering eyes.

"May you never stop noticing"
eyes open excited
offering an evolved wonderment
that could have been missed
while worrying about darkness.

Studying

Studying how thumbs open clay
how fingers steady the urge to lean
too far one way and slump
how tender pressure toward the center
steadies the spinning sides
so they climb together.

Studying how the shore receives
the sea's debris
smooths edges.

Studying how pelicans dive
wings   body   beak   a perfect arrow
how a flock flies in a sideways V
taking turns to lead
keeping the spaces between them even.

Studying how ageing knees keep climbing
but prefer a daily walk along a level field
stepping over gopher holes   broken branches
acorns   new grass
how they can deeply bend to study
a mushroom someone might know how to eat
searching for the words to describe
the lavender shade not seen before today.

Oak Galls

Oak galls have been crushed, soaked, mixed with iron,
salt, and something sticky
to become ink adhering to paper.

How many curious humans have rolled the galls
in their hands wondering what they are good for,
and why they have little dark holes.
Some puddles are blacker than others, someone
noticed, something floating and spongy.

Someone noticed a curling oak leaf, a clinging wet drop,
and later a hard amber ball.
Turns out a wasp's egg cocoons itself
until it's ready to burrow a hole and fly out.

Some humans bit the gall believing it was an apple,
but bitter, way too bitter and tough to swallow.

To have gall means to be too bold, rude,
virulent, brazen; full of bile, liver out of control.

What does it mean that I have been collecting them,
arranging them with acorns, pinecones, and pomegranates;
floating them in a fountain pool with owl feathers as sails?
Am I revealing my obsession with expression,
an irritation seeking a cocoon for transformation,
a beginning insisting on becoming winged?

Floating Oak Galls With Owl Feather Sails

They tip over
I need to reset the feather higher
more to one side
try two feathers
bow and stern.

They scoot across the water
when the wind's from the west
get caught in the corner
the wood boats wedging them together.

I am experimenting with basic science.
Will tipped over wet feathers
fluff up and sail?
Will a predator attack what might be
a baby owl?
Will the crested titmouse be tempted
to balance on a feather as well as
the wide water spout.

What should I try next
wind in my soul
wonder in my mind
possibility in my hand?

Eating Miner's Lettuce

Hungry seekers have scavenged the woods for game,
and peered into flowing water for gold flecks,

and long grasses for a bouquet of green
barely rooted, briefly present.

How did the miners know to eat it?
How do I?

My teaching colleague Marc, called Treebeard,
held it up on one of our hikes and nibbled.

The kids and I tried an edge, the whole thing,
and reached for another, warned to not take too much

so next year, the year after
someone, or an animal could survive:

a deer, a rabbit. We knew we were
related to wildness. Stood still. Were quiet.

Followed Treebeard and his tall walking stick,
looking for what we could point at

to learn how else we could survive,
not starve or die because we didn't

learn how to learn by searching, touching,
tasting. By trusting.

Living With Lizards

Living with lizards chasing each other
crossing tails and shadows
meditating in cobra pose
not moving until my foot almost
lands on their sunning backs

flat bellied on the cement
limbs limp

listening when spoken to
leaning their heads
pumping their torsos
saying nothing

long toes gripping the twisted wisteria vine
quickly climbing up
abruptly heading down
racing under the rosemary to be on the look out
completely relaxed while alert

I tell my mind
tell my body
"You can do that too."

Sun on our skins reflecting
same sun same air.

Dusting The Floor

Dusting the floor with the rug I intend
to shake out the open door
      foxtails, wisteria blossoms,
      mosquito hawks tangled in spider webs.

I warned the little frog escaping behind the washer
      "Don't go there. You'll die in the dust!"

Every year I carry a desiccated frog to the basket of bones,
and de-feathered birds that died trying to fly
through our house with its glass lined up for light.

I spend so much time picking up what has dried,
fallen, stuck to the bottom of a shoe,

time avoiding the big messes people dump
into the news, too much to sweep with the rug,
to drag out the door, shake into the wind

asking it to take it back, turn it into roses and doves.

Wind

Wind can blow all the blossoms off the plum tree
slam a snow drift against a door
rush a fire up a ridge
wreck a cherished home
drive pollen up a sneezing nose
uproot old oaks
raise waves
flood cities
twirl a barn into a neighbor's field

can become a conspiracy of hot rumors
harmonize in a symphony
propel a sail
cool a day's sweat
hum a taut wire

can carry away grief
deliver a scent of cinnamon
garlic   lavender   lemon

can urge a breath to utter a word
to howl anger   shout joy   sigh

can pause for silent listening
for inspiration to sing clearly.

Colliding In Space And Time

A meteor's debris decorates the sky repeatedly
though we can't see it unless we stay up,
clouds don't hover
Jupiter's light is just right and
we long to watch the rare event
to know we did to tell how it felt
to breathe the past reoccurring.

We miss so much. How can we not?
All that emptiness and our clock's insistent scheduling,
but it's worth waking up to witness mystery,
to catch the sparks collision has not extinguished,
to face the dark knowing we did and lived,

like Perseus with Medusa's severed head
that could have turned him into stone.
He had his polished shield, a horse, his destiny
to slay what jealous Athena punished.
He has a constellation named after him.

Where did this myth fall from but the dark
upheaval of feminine ascendance,
the threat to power swords must shatter
to scatter the stories
we seldom see clearly.

Thin Air

Vanished into thin air we say about
            losing   not finding
air so everywhere
            what direction to look
up   around   inside   under

even thin air can be thick
            though not solid
gases floating   flying light struck
            heated   cooled   dry
            fresh   stinky

all that chemistry   elevated numbers
            scary to think we have to
            take in what can make us sick

the thin   invisible dancer   always with us
our lives dependent   on long kisses.

This Small Fly

This small fly is everywhere on me
its current colony
in my hair   on my finger   toe
in my book   on my pen

like the floaters in my eyes
rising   falling   dashing to the right
like my ideas for home and self-improvement
for world peace.

I try to catch it   flick it away
why me now
its continent to explore
curious   compulsive   intimate exploration.

I practice noting my perturbation
questions   violent urges   itches.

Such a little thing
so much attention.

I walk outside into the wind and plead
free us   free us from each other's fixations
whatever we have to learn
let it be now forever amen.

Spider With White Knees

We worry each other.
"I want to free you to live outside the house,
want to free myself from fear of your being in the house."

I reach with a black and white towel,
hit the mouse trap under the fridge,
which flips over not snapping my fingers,
but I rear up and the spider scoots under the fridge.

I feel like a well-meaning fool judging who should
live in this house by the sea we built and rarely visit,
cover the furniture, wipe the counter, lock up and leave

the spiders in peace,
the mice, moths, ants,
the mirrors reflecting the wide sea,
framing the night sky and the horizon,

hosting without preference
a shrouded sunset,
a slow gold and magenta parade,
a flash of green.

Ravens On The Baja Coast

Ravens fly by announcing something urgent,
their presence a startling wonder.

Tongued, gleaming black,
their closed wings are high shoulders, sober robes.

It's easy to call them Your Honors,
to name them morticians,
tricksters, wise ones, tough guys,
sentinels.

Their long beaks lock to secure a twisting snake
on its death flight.

Territorial, they paint our roof with white puddles,
the remains of their frequent repasts.

They are older than anything I know for certain,
a bold contrast to the blue taffeta sea
and the innocent deep mist.

Timidity is not their secret middle name.

Their discovered bleached skull bones and beaks
lean on the seashells lining my windowsill,
their feathers are bookmarks
stroking my cheeks during difficult passages.

We deliberate, declare,
pass considered judgements,
turn the page,
settle in silence.

Asking Nothing

The sea asks nothing
of fish   diving pelicans.

It sways   flows   thins   mirrors.
Thinking is not how it attracts
dreaming and enterprising hands.

The sea sings its hymns
repeating the same stanzas
varying crescendos
erasing silence
rising   easing back
not resisting wind.

The sea often winks
waves white flags
flashes diamonds
not expecting
applause or a response.

Drift Mode

Where I want to be when weary
        no goal to snag a big one
        no pull of anchor
        no hook to bait
        no fish to free from hook in gill
        no net balanced starboard

just being rocked in my own ripples
while day slips into dark
while the moon   whatever her mood is
        floats in and out of fog

alone   listening
seeing   not needing to
        identify   count   compare
        worry   plan   answer   question

breath and breeze
at ease with each other.

Acknowledgments

Most ripples are not noticeable, so many simultaneously occurring, obscuring; so subtle or overwhelming from the past, present, and future's known and imagined places. Some are seen, heard, and felt. Some are sought and saved. These poems emerged during the challenging years of 2016-2022 through conversations, observations, and "bounces" with poets beginning with biweekly meetings with Steve Braff and Teresa MacLean McNeil.

For a while I was "Poet of the Zendo" in the Santa Ynez Valley, a refuge many of us sought to be sane and to learn how to sit still and pay attention, to allow chaos to calm by being open and present. My thanks to Kanjin and my fellow meditators for inviting and welcoming my poems.

I am fortunate to live in beautiful places, the Santa Ynez Valley in California and on the coast of Baja, with a supportive family and good friends, especially my husband Tom Ryder and the Women's Group who care about me and encourage me to write.

Covid contagion forced isolation but sharing poems deepened communication. I am grateful to Brenda Juarez, Rosalind Ruth, Judy Luiz, Sally Mason, Chris DiPego, and Melissa Salmon for provocative prompts and responses.

The writers and artists I know have kept working and inspire me, especially my son Matthew Monahan and daughter-in-law Lara Schnitger who created sculptures, slogans, and garments for Suffragettes' City marches in many cities of Europe and the U.S.

I am especially grateful to Cynthia Carbone Ward who helped select the poems and cheers me on, along with Nyuol Lueth Tong. Jim Kenney and Alicia Dwyer Ryder provided valuable art advice. Matthew Monahan's drawing is on the cover, perfect for the shifting rippling of these poems.

Steve Braff skillfully assisted at the finish. Brenda Juarez has held my hand and been the major designer with patience and impressive power over the computer, enabling my rough drafts to ripple.

About the Author

Dorothy Jardin is an educator, artist, and counselor trained in Council Circle and Hakomi Psychotherapy and a fellow in the South Coast Writing Project at the University of California, Santa Barbara, California. She taught Language Arts and English at Dunn School and works as a group facilitator and a counselor to individuals. Her poems have been published in *The PostSCWriP, The Bell View, Meridian, Foothill Quarterly,* and *Mother's Underground.* She lives with her husband Tom Ryder in Los Olivos, California and in Baja, Mexico and near her grown sons Matthew Monahan and Derek Ryder and their families in Los Angeles, California.

Made in the USA
Las Vegas, NV
19 September 2023

77832836R00050